LADIES IN WAITING

VOL 2

PASSIONATE HEARTS:
HOW DO YOU KNOW HE'S THE ONE?

Dr Lovella Mogere and Collaborative

Ladies In Waiting Vol 2
Copyright © 2024 by Dr Lovella Mogere

ISBN: 9798328882927

Printed in the USA by Nous Mass Media (www.nousmassmedia.com)

TABLE OF CONTENTS

FOREWORD

In the intricate dance of romance, the question "How do you know he's the one?" often becomes a haunting melody, echoing through the hearts and minds of women everywhere. This inquiry is not just about finding a partner but about discovering a profound connection that resonates with the deepest parts of our being.

Ladies In Waiting Vol 2 - Passionate Hearts: "How Do You Know He's The One?" is a heartfelt exploration of this universal question. It delves into the complexities of love, offering guidance and insights to help you recognize the signs of true compatibility. As you turn these pages, you will embark on a journey through the seasons of a relationship, understanding the unique challenges and joys that each phase brings.

In spring, you will feel the thrill of new beginnings, the excitement of discovery, and the promise of potential. Summer will immerse you in the warmth of deepening bonds and shared experiences. Autumn will guide you through periods of reflection and adjustment, while winter will test your endurance and commitment, ultimately leading to renewal and growth.

This book is more than a guide; it is a companion for every woman navigating the labyrinth of love. It blends personal anecdotes with expert advice, creating a tapestry of wisdom that is both relatable and enlightening. The stories and insights within these pages are drawn from real experiences, offering you a genuine and compassionate perspective on what it means to find "the one."

As you read, you will learn to balance the passion of your heart with the wisdom of your head, ensuring that your choices in love are both emotionally fulfilling and logically sound. You will discover how to nurture the seeds of trust, respect, and mutual growth that form the bedrock of a lasting partnership.

Whether you are at the beginning of a new romance, evaluating a long-term relationship, or simply reflecting on your journey in love, **Ladies In Waiting Vol 2 - Passionate Hearts** is here to support and inspire you. It is a testament to the power of love, a celebration of resilience, and a guide to finding a connection that stands the test of time.

In the following chapters, let your heart be open to the possibilities of love, and let your mind be a guiding light in your quest for the one who is truly meant for you. May this book bring you clarity, confidence, and the courage to embrace the love you deserve.

With warmth and hope,

Elizabeth Rawlins

PREFACE

The journey to finding true love is one of the most profound and universal experiences in life. It is filled with moments of joy, doubt, discovery, and growth. In my work and personal life, I have seen countless women grapple with the question: "How do you know he's the one?" This question, simple yet profound, can shape our lives in the most unexpected ways.

Ladies In Waiting Vol 2 - Passionate Hearts: "How Do You Know He's The One?" is born out of a desire to offer guidance and solace to those navigating this complex journey. This book is for every woman who has ever wondered if her partner is her true soulmate, who has ever questioned the depth and longevity of her relationship, and who seeks clarity and confidence in her romantic choices.

Drawing on a rich tapestry of personal anecdotes, expert insights, and timeless wisdom, this book explores the various stages of a relationship. From the initial spark of attraction to the enduring flame of long-term commitment, each chapter delves into the unique challenges and joys that define the journey of love.

You will find practical advice on balancing emotions with logic, understanding the signals of true compatibility, and nurturing a relationship that stands the test of time. This book aims to be a trusted companion, offering you the tools to recognize and cultivate a love that is both passionate and enduring.

As you embark on this journey through the pages of **Ladies In Waiting Vol 2 - Passionate Hearts**, I hope you find the answers you seek and the inspiration to embrace the love you deserve. This book is a testament to the power of love, a celebration of resilience, and a guide to finding a connection that is authentically and uniquely yours.

May your heart be open to the possibilities of love, and may your mind be a guiding light in your quest for the one who is truly meant for you.

With love and gratitude,

Dr Lovella Mogere

INTRODUCTION

Welcome In the labyrinth of love, finding "the one" can feel like an elusive quest. Every woman, at some point in her journey, grapples with the profound question: "How do you know he's the one?" This question is not just about identifying a life partner but about understanding the depths of compatibility, connection, and commitment that define a truly fulfilling relationship.

Ladies In Waiting Vol 2 - Passionate Hearts: "How Do You Know He's The One?" delves into this intricate journey, offering a compass to navigate the winding paths of romance and commitment. This volume is dedicated to every woman who has ever wondered if her partner is her true soulmate. It is a guide through the myriad emotions, doubts, and revelations that accompany the search for lasting love.

Through insightful chapters, personal anecdotes, and expert advice, this book explores the various facets of love and partnership. From the initial sparks of attraction in spring to the deepening bonds of summer, the reflective adjustments of autumn, and the enduring commitment of winter, the narrative mirrors the natural cycles of relationships. Each chapter is crafted to help you recognize the signs of true compatibility and understand the signals that indicate whether your relationship has the potential for lifelong fulfillment.

In this volume, you will find tools to balance the heart's passion with the head's wisdom, ensuring that your decisions in love are both emotionally satisfying and logically sound. You will learn to identify and nurture the seeds of trust, respect, and mutual growth that form the foundation of enduring partnerships.

Whether you are in the throes of a new romance, evaluating a long-term relationship, or simply reflecting on your journey in love, **Ladies In Waiting Vol 2 - Passionate Hearts** provides the insights and encouragement you need. It is a testament to the belief that love, when nurtured with both passion and reason, can flourish and stand the test of time.

Join us as we explore the timeless question of how to recognize "the one" and embark on a journey to a deeper, more fulfilling love. Let this book be your companion as you navigate the beautiful, complex, and ultimately rewarding path of finding and sustaining true love.

CHAPTER ONE

LOVE IN EVERY SEASON: SUSTAINING A LIFELONG PARTNERSHIP

In the journey of life, love is not a static entity but a dynamic force that evolves through different seasons. Just as nature experiences the changing tides of spring, summer, autumn, and winter, so too does a lifelong partnership go through its own cycles of growth, challenges, and renewal. Understanding and navigating these seasons is crucial for sustaining a deep and meaningful connection.

Spring: The Season of New Beginnings

Spring in a relationship is marked by the freshness of new beginnings and the budding of emotions. It's a time of excitement, discovery, and laying the foundation for what's to come. Couples in this season often experience a heightened sense of passion, curiosity about each other, and a willingness to explore and learn together. Communication is key during this phase as partners set expectations, establish boundaries, and build trust.

To sustain a lifelong partnership, it's essential to nurture the seeds planted in spring. This involves open and honest communication, actively listening to each other's needs, and being willing to adapt and grow together. Just as spring nourishes the earth, investing time and effort into the relationship during this season lays the groundwork for a strong and resilient connection.

Summer: The Season of Growth and Fulfillment

As relationships mature, they enter the summer season—a time of growth, warmth, and fulfillment. Partners in this phase experience a deepening of their bond, a sense of companionship, and the joy of shared experiences. They may find comfort in each other's presence, develop routines, and navigate life's challenges as a team.

During summer, sustaining a lifelong partnership involves fostering intimacy and building a sense of partnership. This includes celebrating successes together, supporting each other through setbacks, and continually finding ways to keep the relationship vibrant and fulfilling. It's about cherishing the moments spent together and appreciating the strengths and unique qualities each partner brings to the union.

Autumn: The Season of Reflection and Adjustment

Autumn brings with it a time of reflection and adjustment in a relationship. As partners navigate the complexities of life, they may encounter changes in priorities, interests, and personal growth. This season challenges couples to adapt to new circumstances, revisit goals, and redefine their roles within the relationship.

To sustain a lifelong partnership during autumn, it's important to embrace change with empathy and understanding. This includes communicating openly about evolving needs, respecting individual identities, and finding common ground amidst differences. Nurturing mutual respect and practicing forgiveness can help couples weather the challenges of this season and emerge stronger together.

Winter: The Season of Renewal and Endurance

Winter in a relationship symbolizes a time of endurance, reflection, and renewal. Couples may face challenges such as loss, aging, or transitions that test their resilience and commitment. It's a season that requires patience, empathy, and a willingness to weather storms together.

To sustain a lifelong partnership during winter, it's crucial to prioritize emotional support, maintain a sense of humor, and cultivate gratitude for the journey shared. This season offers an opportunity for deepening emotional intimacy, rediscovering shared values, and reaffirming the bond that has endured through the seasons.

Conclusion

Love in every season is about embracing the ebb and flow of life's journey together. It's about navigating transitions with grace, celebrating milestones with joy, and supporting each other through the inevitable challenges that arise. By understanding the unique characteristics of each season—spring's beginnings, summer's growth, autumn's adjustments, and winter's endurance—couples can cultivate a lifelong partnership filled with love, resilience, and lasting happiness.

Additionally, finding community and solidarity with other Black women who share similar experiences can provide validation, support, and collective strength in the journey towards authenticity. By uplifting each other's voices and amplifying our truths, we can create spaces of empowerment and liberation where our identities are celebrated and honored.

Reclaiming our authenticity requires courage, resilience, and a commitment to living in alignment with our deepest truths. It is an ongoing process of self-discovery and self-affirmation, but one that is essential for our mental, emotional, and spiritual well-being. By embracing our authentic selves and refusing to be defined by society's narrow expectations, we can forge a path towards greater wholeness, fulfillment, and liberation.

Discussion Questions

Spring: New Beginnings

What are the key characteristics of the "spring" season in a relationship, according to the author? How do these characteristics contribute to laying a strong foundation for a lifelong partnership?

Why is open and honest communication emphasized during the spring phase? How does effective communication set the stage for future growth and intimacy?

Summer: Growth and Fulfillment

Describe the "summer" season in a relationship. What are the signs that a couple has entered this phase? How does shared experience contribute to deepening the bond between partners?

What strategies can couples employ to maintain intimacy and fulfillment during the summer season? How does celebrating successes and supporting each other through challenges strengthen the relationship?

Autumn: Reflection and Adjustment

In what ways does the "autumn" season challenge couples to adapt and grow? How do changing priorities and personal growth influence the dynamics of a lifelong partnership?

How can couples navigate differences and evolving needs during the autumn phase? What role does empathy, respect, and forgiveness play in sustaining the relationship through this season?

Winter: Renewal and Endurance

What does the "winter" season symbolize in a relationship? How do challenges such as loss or transitions test the resilience of couples?

What practical steps can couples take to prioritize emotional support and strengthen their commitment during the winter season? How does enduring challenges together deepen emotional intimacy?

Conclusion: Embracing Life's Journey

Reflecting on the entire lifecycle of a relationship described by Lovella, what lessons can individuals draw about the nature of love and partnership?

How does understanding and embracing the ebb and flow of life's journey together contribute to the longevity and happiness of a lifelong partnership?

Personal Reflection and Application

Based on the discussion of each season, how can individuals apply the insights from "Love in Every Season" to their own relationships or future relationships?

What are some practical strategies or habits that individuals can adopt to cultivate a relationship that evolves and thrives through different seasons of life?

Challenges and Opportunities

What are some potential challenges couples may face in recognizing and navigating through the different seasons of their relationship?

How can couples turn these challenges into opportunities for growth, understanding, and deeper connection?

BIO

Dr. Lovella Mogere is the CEO of Leaders Who Lead Differently, a pioneering organization dedicated to unlocking the DNA of Cultural Innovation. As a leader of leaders, Lovella spearheads multiple movements aimed at guiding leaders towards succession, empowering them to navigate the complexities of an ever-changing world.

With a global perspective and an entrepreneurial spirit, Lovella is renowned as a thought leader who catalyzes transformative change. Her visionary leadership style transcends borders, inspiring individuals, and organizations to embrace innovation and embrace the infinite possibilities within their reach.

As an international speaker and best-selling author, Lovella shares her insights and expertise on leadership, cultural innovation, and the power of mindset shifts. Through her dynamic presentations and influential writings, she challenges conventional thinking and ignites a passion for continuous growth and evolution.

To learn more about Dr. Lovella Mogere and her work, visit www.lovellamogere.com and embark on a journey of discovery, empowerment, and transformation.

CHAPTER TWO

MARRIAGE IN SPIRIT AND IN TRUTH

Marriage is a divine institution that, when approached with reverence and obedience to God's Word, completes the fruitfulness of worship. It offers a platform for wives to grow spiritually together with their husbands, enabling you to support one another in your journey in Christ. Just as the Kingdom of God thrives on unity and mutual support, respect, service and honor among believers, a God-centered marriage contributes to the expansion of His Kingdom on Earth.

Wives, remember your assignment in marriage is first dedicated to the servanthood and honor of the King, and His Kingdom and in return you, as a joint heir of that Kingdom, receive the FULL benefits and rite-of-passage of the blessing of the Lord! The blessing being that of wholeness, newness, health wealth healing and provision of peace. Not by the Hand of your husband, but by the Hand of God through your husband.

In God's design, marriage is a sacred covenant that mirrors the unity and completeness of the Kingdom of God. By embracing the process of two becoming one in marriage, individuals fulfill their purpose as worshippers and obedient servants of the Lord. Through this divine union, they contribute to the fruitfulness of God's Kingdom, bringing glory to His name and sharing in the abundant blessings of His design for marriage.

Discussion Questions

Understanding the Divine Institution of Marriage:

How does viewing marriage as a divine institution change your perspective on the role and responsibilities within a marriage?

____

____

____

____

____

In what ways does a God-centered marriage contribute to the fruitfulness of worship and the expansion of His Kingdom on Earth?

____

____

____

____

____

Role of Wives in a God-Centered Marriage:

What does it mean for a wife's assignment in marriage to be dedicated to the servanthood and honor of the King and His Kingdom?

____

____

____

____

____

How can wives support their husbands spiritually and contribute to their joint journey in Christ?

____

____

____

____

Receiving God's Blessings Through Marriage:

How does the concept of receiving blessings from God through your husband influence the dynamic of a Christian marriage?

Discuss the idea that blessings such as wholeness, health, and peace come by the Hand of God rather than solely from the husband.

Unity and Covenant in Marriage:

In what ways does the unity of two becoming one in marriage mirror the unity and completeness of the Kingdom of God?

How can couples embrace this process to fulfill their purpose as worshippers and obedient servants of the Lord?

Marriage as a Reflection of God's Kingdom:

How does a sacred covenant in marriage reflect the principles of unity, mutual support, respect, service, and honor among believers in the Kingdom of God?

What practical steps can couples take to ensure their marriage contributes to bringing glory to God's name and sharing in His abundant blessings?

Spiritual Growth in Marriage:

How can a couple actively grow spiritually together in their marriage, and what practices can help support this growth?

What challenges might arise in maintaining a God-centered marriage, and how can couples overcome these challenges through faith and obedience?

Role of Servanthood and Honor:

How can embracing the roles of servanthood and honor within marriage enhance the spiritual and emotional bond between spouses?

In what ways can husbands and wives mutually support each other in their individual and joint callings within the marriage?

Impact of a God-Centered Marriage on the Community:

How can the principles of a God-centered marriage extend beyond the couple to impact their family, church, and broader community?

What examples can you share of marriages that have positively influenced others by embodying the values discussed in this chapter?

____

____

____

____

Personal Reflection and Application:

Reflect on your own marriage or future marriage aspirations. How can you apply the principles of a God-centered marriage to your relationship?

____

____

____

____

____

What specific steps can you take to ensure that your marriage aligns with the vision of "Marriage in Spirit and in Truth" as described in this chapter?

____

____

____

____

Challenges and Rewards of a God-Centered Marriage:

What are some common challenges that couples might face when striving to maintain a God-centered marriage, and how can they address these challenges?

Discuss the rewards and blessings that come from approaching marriage with reverence and obedience to God's Word. How have you experienced these rewards in your own life or observed them in others?

BIO

 Dr. Carmen Nicolle McKnight-Judie is a Wife and mother of three. She has been Commissioned by the Lord God and called into prophetic ministry. She is a teacher of the Word and has a deep love and passion for Gods people to be restored and reconciled in every area of their life. She is an Apostolic Prophet and Prophetic Teacher in the Word and Worship Arts.

She is the Founder and Creative Director of Breath of Fire Ministry In The Arts. "Breath Of Fire" is a Prophetic School of Worship Located in Houston, Tx. Carmen is also the Founder and Dean of an online mentoring academy called "Identity N` Truth", and the founder of "Strike The Ground" A Apostolic and Prophetic Training Hub for Intercessors.

To Learn More About the Ministry That was given to her, please visit: Website: www.Breathoffireministry.org.

Email: tmills72@gmail.com
Facebook: www.facebook.com/Bofmota
Online Mentoring: www.identityntruth.thinkific.com
Facebook Mentoring Group:
www.facebook.com/groups/IdentityNTruth
Facebook training for intercession:
Www.facebook.com. /groups/striketheground

CHAPTER THREE

YOU FIT INTO EACH OTHER'S LIVES REALLY WELL

We know the story of Adam awakened by God when He brought Eve to him, but have you considered God's reasoning? The Lord God says, "It is not good that the man should be alone, I will make him an help meet for him" (Gen 2:18). No beast or fowl was a fit, but Eve was a perfect fit. The moment Adam saw Eve, he knew she was a fit for his life. Adam proclaimed, "She is bone of my bones and flesh of my flesh: she shall be called Woman" (Gen 2:23). In the natural sense, the bone represents support, and the flesh represents wholeness. Basically, the woman should be the support and wholeness to the man; fitting really well with her heart.

When fixing your crown while waiting on God to present you to your husband, don't forget to fix your heart. Your heart needs to be soft, to be the support and wholeness that your husband will need. I'm not speaking from a level of I had my heart right, no I failed multiple times in marriages, but I'm speaking from a level of my willingness to fix my heart. Because of my willingness, God presented me to my husband. Ultimately, his perfect fit; support and wholeness in the Lord.

I will never forget the time my husband said to me, "You're not being patient with me." Those words hit me to my core, my heart. It was at that moment, I knew I was not just his wife, but his woman and his help meet. With those words ringing in my ears, my heart began to soften. For me to be patient, I needed to suffer long by putting aside my motives so that I may fit in with his life; keywords: his life. The Lord God had already presented me to him. My husband already saw me as his support and wholeness, but I needed to become his bone and flesh. You can dishonor your role to your husband and the Lord God by picking which fruits you choose to bear. When you dishonor, you will cause the support and wholeness to break; thus, creating fragmentation-like puzzles that do not fit your God-ordained marriage.

How do you know you two fit well into each other's lives? When the two of you are willing to pray to God as one for the unmet needs. Personally, if my husband hasn't met my need, I've learned that I have to go to the Lord God in prayer. And, I have to wait on the Lord God to drop it in my husband's spirit. Whether you want to or not; you still have to wait in your marriage. This is why you want to be intentional in being the best fit, meaning suitable to your husband through your heart. Remember, "The heart of her husband doth safely trust in her, so that he shall have no need of spoil" (Prov 31:11).

Discussion Questions

Understanding the Concept of 'Help Meet:

How do you interpret the term "help meet" as described in Genesis 2:18? What does it mean for a woman to be a perfect fit for her husband in the context of this passage?

In what ways can women today embody the role of support and wholeness in their marriages?

The Importance of a Soft Heart:

How does having a soft heart contribute to being a supportive and whole partner in a marriage?

Can you share a personal experience where softening your heart made a positive difference in your relationship?

Patience and Understanding in Marriage:

Reflect on the statement, "You're not being patient with me." How can patience impact the dynamics of a marriage?

What practical steps can couples take to cultivate patience and understanding towards each other?

Role of Prayer in Strengthening Marriage:

Discuss the importance of praying together as a couple. How does this practice help in aligning unmet needs and strengthening the bond between spouses?

How can individuals approach God in prayer when their needs are not being met by their partner, and what should their mindset be during this waiting period?

Maintaining Trust and Intentionality:

How can wives ensure that their husbands' hearts safely trust in them, as mentioned in Proverbs 31:11?

What does it mean to be intentional in being the best fit for your husband, and how can wives practice this intentionality in their daily lives?

Learning from Marital Failures:

The author mentions failing multiple times in marriages before finding success. How can individuals learn from past relationship failures to improve their current or future marriages?

Discuss the role of self-reflection and willingness to change in overcoming marital challenges.

Support and Wholeness:

How do the concepts of bone (support) and flesh (wholeness) translate into practical actions within a marriage?

What are some ways spouses can actively support and make each other feel whole in their daily interactions?

Dealing with Fragmentation:

What are some signs that support and wholeness are breaking down in a marriage, and how can couples address these issues before they lead to fragmentation?

How can couples work together to ensure their marriage remains a fitting and harmonious partnership?

Personal Growth and Marital Harmony:

How does focusing on personal growth and heart transformation contribute to the overall harmony and success of a marriage?

What are some strategies individuals can use to continuously improve themselves and, in turn, their marriage?

Scriptural Guidance:

How can the scriptures and principles have discussed in this chapter guide couples in their journey to becoming a perfect fit for each other?

Share some biblical passages that have personally helped you in your marriage or relationship and explain how they influenced your actions and decisions.

BIO

Jannie Booker has served the Lord for over 20 years. God has entrusted her in many areas of ministry from preaching in the pulpit, conference speaking, to evangelizing the streets.

Jannie holds no punches in Ministry. She speaks with such boldness and passion to motivate believers, equip the Saints in prayer, and win souls for the Lord Jesus Christ. It was once said that 'if she was selling Jesus, I would buy Him.' Jannie has been a member of The Gospel of Jesus Christ Church since 2005 and ordained a Minister in 2010 under the leadership of Bishop Dr. Castile Colbert, Jr. and his wife Minister Vanessa Colbert. Jannie is the founder of PSST Pure Simple Sincere True broadcast, where life situations are conversed. Jannie's power gifts from the Lord are in intercession and preaching.

The Lord has gifted her with prophetic intercession under the leadership of her mentor Tonya Brown. Jannie Booker is married, has 3 children, and 2 grandchildren. Jannie holds two Masters Degrees, and works as a Registered Nurse.

Facebook: https://www.facebook.com/Sis.Jannie

CHAPTER FOUR

DIVINE PREPARATION: A JOURNEY TO FINDING MY GOD-GIVEN SPOUSE

Before I could be in a place of being able to receive my GOD given spouse, the one that I was created for, I had to be prepared mentally, spiritually, and even physically. I had to go through a cleansing stage, a stage where it was only myself and GOD.

When you have given of yourself repeatedly to the wrong man, at some point we have to take a retrospective look at ourselves and ask GOD to shine the light in on and all throughout us. In this process, we are awakened to the counterfeits posed as soul mates. These people are nothing more than a mere distraction. Being divorced for some time before my GOD ordained one found me, I decided I would not settle for less, nor would I just accept anything. I was well over my forties, and some were already side eying me regarding celibacy and my waiting. I can't sit up here and tell you all those who came in the name of GOD and in the name of lust but were sent to try to derail me. Since I was married before, I knew what I was willing to accept, and what would not work for me.

No matter what the counterfeits, I kept working while waiting. I was excited about getting my relationship with GOD and myself in order. Staying active in church, having positive relationships with other singles, and not mingling with those who were still doing things I had been delivered from, was very helpful and aided me in my waiting period. I, myself after year six of celibacy, was like, "Okay GOD, if marriage is not in your will for me, I will still obey?"

I went through what I would like to call a death to self and death to flesh so that I could live all over again. There was a soul tie separation that had to be conquered so all previous attachments would be destroyed. I made a vow to God and myself that I would not be the same person and that I would rid myself of every old way that kept me bound and that kept me from progressing and moving forward in loving and being loved the correct way along with being able to receive the love properly without holding on to the past. In my waiting, I gave myself in totality to being made whole.

When I met my husband, I knew that it was something different about him during our dating period. I knew he was the one and within five months, God allowed us both to know this was it and we were married, working for God together. It was not forced, but it was ordained and set in stone by God. I admonish you to never settle, stay prayerful, and allow God to be the center of your life. Allow God to choose and always remember that every good and perfect gift comes from God.

Discussion Questions

The Role of Preparation:

How did the author's mental, spiritual, and physical preparation influence her ability to recognize and receive her God-given spouse?

Why is it important to go through a cleansing stage where it is just oneself and God? How can this stage impact one's future relationships?

____

____

____

____

Identifying Counterfeits:

What are some signs or red flags that can help individuals identify counterfeits posing as soul mates?

____

____

____

____

____

How can past relationships and experiences help in distinguishing between a genuine partner and a counterfeit?

____

____

____

____

____

Maintaining Standards and Celibacy:

How did maintaining high standards and practicing celibacy benefit the author during her waiting period?

____

____

What challenges might one face when deciding not to settle for less, and how can they overcome societal pressures or judgments?

Importance of Positive Relationships:

How did staying active in church and maintaining positive relationships with other singles support the author during her waiting period?

Why is it crucial to avoid mingling with individuals who engage in behaviors from which one has been delivered?

Death to Self and Flesh:

What does the author mean by going through a "death to self and death to flesh" to live all over again?

How can one effectively break soul ties and detach from previous attachments to become whole?

Vowing to Change and Being Made Whole:

How did the author's vow to God and herself to not remain the same person contribute to her personal growth and readiness for a new relationship?

In what ways can giving oneself to being made whole prepare an individual for a healthy, God-centered relationship?

Recognizing the Right Partner:

What factors or feelings helped the author recognize that her husband was the right one during their dating period?

How can one discern if a relationship is ordained and set in stone by God?

Prayer and Obedience:

How did staying prayerful and obedient to God's will guide the author in her journey to finding her spouse?

Why is it important to allow God to choose one's partner rather than relying solely on personal judgment?

____

____

____

____

____

Living and Working Together for God:

How did the author and her husband integrate their faith into their marriage and work together for God?

____

____

____

____

____

What are some practical ways couples can ensure that their relationship remains God-centered and aligned with His purposes?

____

____

____

____

____

Advice for Those Waiting:

What advice does the author give to those who are in their waiting period for a God-given spouse?

____

____

How can individuals stay motivated and faithful during extended periods of waiting for the right partner?

BIO

Toya Guerrero is a Woman of GOD who takes Ministry and Sisterhood to heart. This is her second collaborative project as she loves to write.

Email: tmills72@gmail.com
Facebook: www.facebook.com/toyapraise.mills

CHAPTER FIVE

FELL IN LUST

Lust is defined as "an intense longing" I found myself in lust rather than love. In a season of my life, I was so far away from God. I was drinking, smoking, partying, and dating without purpose. I was going on dates every day of the week, with someone new. Some nights, I ended up waking up to someone I knew wasn't the one for me!

Love is silence, Lust is roar. Love is patient, Lust is moving fast! I have many prophecies of the man of God has for me. Every guy, I was meeting, had me questioning, "Is he the one?" Now, sometimes I would ask God if he's not the one to remove him! A couple of days, sometimes hours later, they would go ghost. It wasn't until I got back into alignment with God, through prayer and fasting that I realize, I was dealing with the spirit of lust.

Longing for something that I desire (Love) on this journey of love, I had many heartaches, disappointment, and just failing in love. When the one God has for you shows up in your life, you won't have to question if he or she is the one God has for you. I thought I failed at love because of so many bad experiences. But, in many situations that made me look at myself differently. I was done with dating at that point. However, I realized I needed to date up. Not lowering my standards for someone that doesn't deserve me. I learned, I don't have run from the fear of rejection, because I've been rejected too many times.

My worth and value has increased. I learned, and I challenge you to take your time deciding and don't rush when making that decision. When you see yourself how God sees you, your desires will change.

Discussion Questions

Understanding Lust vs. Love:

According to the author, what are the defining characteristics of lust versus love?

How did the author distinguish between the two in her personal experiences?

How can individuals prevent themselves from falling into patterns of lust in their relationships?

Personal Journey Away from God:

Describe the author's journey away from God, involving activities like drinking, smoking, partying, and purposeless dating. What impact did this period have on her spiritual and emotional well-being?

How did the author recognize the need to realign herself with God through prayer and fasting? What role did spiritual practices play in her journey back to faith?

Recognizing the Spirit of Lust:

What are some signs or behaviors that indicate one is dealing with the spirit of lust rather than genuine love?

How did the author's realization about lust impact her approach to dating and relationships moving forward?

Dealing with Heartache and Disappointment:

Reflect on the author's experiences of heartache and disappointment in her pursuit of love. How did these experiences shape her perspective on relationships and self-worth?

How can individuals recover from past relationship failures and use them as opportunities for personal growth?

Learning from Rejection:

Discuss the author's view on rejection and its role in her journey. How did repeated rejection influence her approach to dating and self-esteem?

What advice would the author give to someone struggling with the fear of rejection in relationships?

Increasing Self-Worth and Value:

How did the author's journey lead to an increase in her self-worth and value? What steps did she take to recognize her own worthiness independent of others' opinions?

How can individuals cultivate a sense of self-worth and value that is not dependent on external validation or relationships?

Dating with Purpose and Standards:

What does it mean to "date up" and how did this concept impact the author's dating life and standards?

How can individuals maintain their standards in dating without compromising their values or self-respect?

Transformation Through Self-Reflection:

How did the author's self-perception change as she aligned herself with God's view of her?

What lessons can be drawn from her journey of self-reflection and personal growth?

What practical steps can individuals take to align their desires and decisions with God's will for their relationships?

Encouragement and Advice for Others:

Based on the author's experiences, what advice would she give to others who may be struggling with similar challenges in their love lives?

How can individuals foster a healthy and balanced approach to seeking romantic relationships while prioritizing their spiritual and emotional well-being?

Impact of Personal Transformation:

How did the author's transformation impact her outlook on love and relationships?

In what ways did her renewed perspective lead to positive changes in her life?

BIO

April April Greene was born and raised in Canton, MS. April moved to Houston, Texas; August of 2017. Houston was a launching pad to activate the gifts that were already within her. April Greene is the founder of AMGreene Enterprises, LLC. April is a relentless, go-getter. She will not rest until the vision God gave her is fulfilled. She is a single mother that use her gift of networking to create a line of income to not only feed her daughter but to build herself out of poverty. April is a interior design consultant, childcare specialist, and three time best-selling author of her books, "Prayers for the Boss Babes"Vol.1 , "Prayers for the Boss Babes: Caution she doesn't PRAY fair, and "Women for Women" Devotional. She also has released her latest book, "Ladies in Waiting" Sis, Fix your crown!

April has triumphed what statistics said about her.

"Life has not been easy but for those who strive to live a life with God, it never is. With all of this in mind continuing to strive for excellence and with that it led me down several roads that did not always have the smoothest travels, definitely a pothole or two. All routes that I have taken thus far and in the future are to develop a legacy one for and in honor of my daughter."

"Your story, It's not over… it has only begun and even in the darkest of times there is always light"

Email: aprilmgreene34@gmail.com
Website: https://amginteriordesigns.as.me/schedule/c91966af

CHAPTER SIX

LOSS AND FOUND

To the women, know who you are, so you'll know if he's the one. My chapter in the book Ladies in Waiting Vol 2 is titled "Loss and Found." This title signifies hope, change, and progress for women in waiting. The word "loss" is a noun that signifies the act or process of losing, implying that change is possible. Reading snippets of my life might make one think I have endured or should have endured much loss, and they'd be right. However, that isn't where my story ends. My journey extends far beyond its starting point, with hope and prayers guiding the way.

As Christians, we often believe that bad things won't happen, setting ourselves up for failure. I see it differently: I expect bad things to happen, which prepares me for failure and disappointment, all while believing that God's got me.

What inspired me to write this chapter? I held onto the knowledge that someone out there is experiencing something similar and is looking for a reason to hang on. I hope that after reading my journey, someone will realize that their sacrifice is not in vain and that there is life on the other side of the rainbow. In each life, a little rain must fall. And yes, sometimes it feels more like a hurricane, but I promise, because God promised, you will get through it.

What did I learn when writing this chapter? Simply put, that "I am a badass chick." Surviving everything, I went through for as long as I did has taught me that there is life on the other side. I learned that if I stand on all the hurt and pain, allowing it to mold me into a better and stronger person, I can be prepared for the next plateau of my life. There is no testimony without a test, no victory without being a victim. Ultimately, I learned that I am an overcomer.

Discussion Questions

Understanding Loss and Change:

How does the concept that loss signifies the possibility of change resonate with your own experiences of loss?

Can you share an example from your life where a significant loss led to positive change or growth?

Faith and Realistic Expectations:

How do you reconcile the belief that "God's got me" with the expectation that bad things will happen?

How does this approach to faith influence your ability to handle adversity?

____

____

____

____

Inspiration and Empathy:

What parts of the author's journey did you find most inspiring, and why?

____

____

____

____

How can sharing personal stories of struggle help others who are going through similar experiences?

____

____

____

____

Learning from Adversity:

What lessons have you learned from your own experiences of hardship that have shaped who you are today?

____

____

How can embracing the pain and challenges in your life make you stronger and better prepared for the future?

Self-Discovery and Empowerment:

What does it mean to you to be a "badass chick" in the context of overcoming personal challenges?

How has realizing your own strength and resilience impacted your approach to relationships and personal goals?

The Role of Hope and Prayer:

How have hope and prayer played a role in your journey through difficult times?

In what ways can maintaining hope and faith during struggles lead to a more fulfilling life?

Victory and Testimony:

How do you interpret the statement "there is no testimony without a test, no victory without being a victim" in your own life?

Can you share a personal story where a significant challenge ultimately led to a meaningful victory or testimony?

Support Systems and Community:

How important is having a support system during times of struggle, and who have been your key supporters?

In what ways can a community of faith and like-minded individuals provide strength and encouragement during tough times?

BIO

Who is Jo-Anne Blanchard, you ask? She is the down-to-earth girl next door, the kind of person who has never met a stranger. Jo-Anne is a public speaker, poet, inspirationist, owner of Caribbean Affairs T.V., and a dedicated community activist.

She is a proud single mother of four beautiful adults and loves being a grandmother. When you first meet her, you are greeted with a smile so warm that it feels like you've known her forever. An optimist by nature and a dreamer at heart, Jo-Anne's positive outlook on life is infectious. Meeting her will leave you forever changed, inspired to conquer every dream you've ever dared to dream.

If that isn't enough, Jo-Anne is also the host of the show Inside/Out, a radio personality on Movements I-Radio, and a Best-Selling Author. When asked what she likes to do for fun, she replies: decorate, dream, and travel.

Facebook: https://www.facebook.com/joanne.blanchard.79

CHAPTER SEVEN

SIGNS AND SIGNALS: RECOGNIZING TRUE COMPATIBILITY

In the realm of relationships, true compatibility is more than just shared interests or physical attraction; it encompasses a deeper connection that resonates on emotional, intellectual, and even spiritual levels. Recognizing these signs and signals of compatibility is crucial for building a fulfilling and lasting partnership.

Understanding Emotional Compatibility

Emotional compatibility forms the foundation of a healthy relationship. It involves understanding and respecting each other's emotions, responding empathetically to feelings, and feeling secure in expressing vulnerability. Couples who are emotionally compatible often find comfort and support in each other during times of stress or joy. Signs of emotional compatibility include:

Empathy and Understanding: Partners demonstrate a genuine interest in each other's feelings and perspectives, validating emotions without judgment.

Effective Communication: They communicate openly and honestly, both in times of harmony and conflict, fostering trust and intimacy.

Shared Values: They align on core beliefs and priorities, such as family, ethics, and life goals, which provides a sense of unity and direction in the relationship.

Intellectual Stimulation and Compatibility

Intellectual compatibility revolves around engaging conversations, shared interests in learning, and respecting each other's intellect and ideas. It involves stimulating each other's minds, challenging perspectives, and enjoying mutual curiosity. Signs of intellectual compatibility include:

Engaging Conversations: Partners enjoy discussing various topics, exchanging ideas, and learning from each other's insights.

Respect for Differences: They appreciate each other's unique perspectives, fostering an environment where differing opinions are valued and respected.

Mutual Growth: They inspire each other to learn and grow intellectually, whether through reading, exploring new hobbies, or pursuing personal and professional development.

Physical and Sexual Compatibility

Physical and sexual compatibility plays a significant role in a romantic relationship, encompassing both attraction and intimacy. It involves not only physical chemistry but also a mutual understanding and respect for each other's needs and desires. Signs of physical and sexual compatibility include:

Physical Attraction: There is a strong physical attraction and desire towards each other, which enhances intimacy and emotional connection.

Communication about Needs: Partners feel comfortable discussing their preferences, boundaries, and desires openly and respectfully.

Mutual Satisfaction: They prioritize each other's pleasure and satisfaction, creating a safe and fulfilling sexual relationship that evolves over time.

Spiritual and Lifestyle Compatibility

Spiritual and lifestyle compatibility refers to shared beliefs, practices, and lifestyle choices that align harmoniously within the relationship. It involves respecting each other's spiritual journey, supporting personal growth, and navigating life's challenges with shared values. Signs of spiritual and lifestyle compatibility include:

Shared Beliefs: Partners share similar spiritual beliefs, or they respect and support each other's individual spiritual paths.

Lifestyle Alignment: They have compatible lifestyles in terms of health, leisure activities, financial values, and long-term goals.

Supportive Partnership: They encourage each other's personal growth and well-being, fostering a supportive environment where both partners can thrive.

Conclusion

Recognizing true compatibility is a journey of self-discovery and mutual understanding. It involves acknowledging and appreciating the unique qualities that each partner brings to the relationship while nurturing a connection that evolves and strengthens over time. By understanding the signs and signals of emotional, intellectual, physical, and spiritual compatibility, couples can cultivate a deep and meaningful partnership that stands the test of time, bringing joy, fulfillment, and resilience to their lives together.

Discussion Questions

Emotional Compatibility:

How important is emotional compatibility in a relationship, according to the article? What are some signs that indicate partners are emotionally compatible?

Can emotional compatibility be developed over time, or is it primarily something that partners either have or don't have from the beginning?

Intellectual Compatibility:

What role does intellectual stimulation play in fostering a deep connection between partners? How can differences in intellectual interests or capacities contribute positively to a relationship?

Share examples of how intellectual compatibility can enhance communication and mutual understanding in a partnership.

Physical and Sexual Compatibility:

Discuss the significance of physical and sexual compatibility in a relationship. How can partners ensure they maintain a healthy and fulfilling physical connection over the long term?

What are some challenges couples might face in achieving and maintaining physical and sexual compatibility? How can these challenges be addressed?

Spiritual and Lifestyle Compatibility:

Why is spiritual and lifestyle compatibility important for the long-term success of a relationship? How can partners navigate differences in spiritual beliefs or practices while maintaining harmony?

In what ways does lifestyle alignment contribute to a sense of unity and shared purpose within a partnership?

Reflecting on Personal Relationships:

Reflect on your own relationships or those you admire. Which aspects of compatibility—emotional, intellectual, physical, or spiritual—do you believe are most critical for sustaining a fulfilling partnership? Why?

Have you experienced challenges related to compatibility in your relationships? How did you navigate them, and what did you learn from those experiences?

Cultivating Compatibility:

What strategies can individuals and couples use to cultivate or strengthen different aspects of compatibility in their relationships?

How can self-awareness and self-improvement contribute to better compatibility with a partner?

Conclusion:

According to the article, how does recognizing true compatibility contribute to the overall happiness and resilience of a relationship?

What advice would you give to someone seeking to assess and enhance compatibility in their current or future relationships, based on the insights shared in this discussion?

These questions aim to facilitate a thoughtful exploration of the different dimensions of compatibility in relationships, encouraging participants to reflect on their own experiences and perspectives while considering practical strategies for building and sustaining fulfilling partnerships.

BIO

 Dr. Lovella Mogere is the CEO of Leaders Who Lead Differently, a pioneering organization dedicated to unlocking the DNA of Cultural Innovation. As a leader of leaders, Lovella spearheads multiple movements aimed at guiding leaders towards succession, empowering them to navigate the complexities of an ever-changing world.

With a global perspective and an entrepreneurial spirit, Lovella is renowned as a thought leader who catalyzes transformative change. Her visionary leadership style transcends borders, inspiring individuals, and organizations to embrace innovation and embrace the infinite possibilities within their reach.

As an international speaker and best-selling author, Lovella shares her insights and expertise on leadership, cultural innovation, and the power of mindset shifts. Through her dynamic presentations and influential writings, she challenges conventional thinking and ignites a passion for continuous growth and evolution.

To learn more about Dr. Lovella Mogere and her work, visit www.lovellamogere.com and embark on a journey of discovery, empowerment, and transformation.

CHAPTER EIGHT

NAVIGATING DOUBT: IS HE THE RIGHT FIT?

Doubt can be a natural part of any relationship journey, especially when considering whether someone is the right life partner. It's a complex question that involves introspection, communication, and careful consideration of various factors. Navigating doubt requires a balanced approach of listening to your instincts while also evaluating the relationship objectively.

Understanding Your Doubts

Doubts in a relationship can stem from various sources, such as conflicting values, communication challenges, or unresolved emotional issues. It's essential to identify the specific concerns causing doubt and reflect on whether they are temporary challenges or fundamental incompatibilities. Some common doubts include:

Compatibility Concerns: Reflecting on whether your values, goals, and lifestyles align in the long term.
Communication Issues: Evaluating how effectively you and your partner communicate and resolve conflicts.
Emotional Connection: Assessing the depth of emotional intimacy and compatibility.
Trust and Respect: Considering whether trust and mutual respect are consistently maintained.

Reflecting on Your Feelings

Take time to reflect on your feelings and intuition about the relationship. Trust your instincts and acknowledge any recurring doubts or concerns. Journaling or discussing your feelings with a trusted friend or therapist can provide clarity and perspective. Ask yourself:

How do I feel when I'm with my partner?

Do I feel respected, valued, and supported?

What are my long-term goals, and do they align with my partner's?

Open and Honest Communication

Effective communication is key to navigating doubts in a relationship. Share your thoughts and feelings with your partner in a calm and constructive manner. Expressing concerns can foster deeper understanding and create opportunities for growth and resolution. Some communication tips include:

Use "I" Statements: Share your feelings and thoughts without placing blame.

Active Listening: Listen attentively to your partner's perspective and validate their feelings.

Problem-Solving Together: Collaborate on finding solutions or compromises that address your doubts.

Seeking Clarity Together

Navigating doubt often involves seeking clarity together as a couple. Have open discussions about your relationship's future, expectations, and concerns. Ask questions that promote understanding and insight, such as:

What are your long-term goals and aspirations?

How do you envision our relationship evolving over time?

What steps can we take to strengthen our connection?

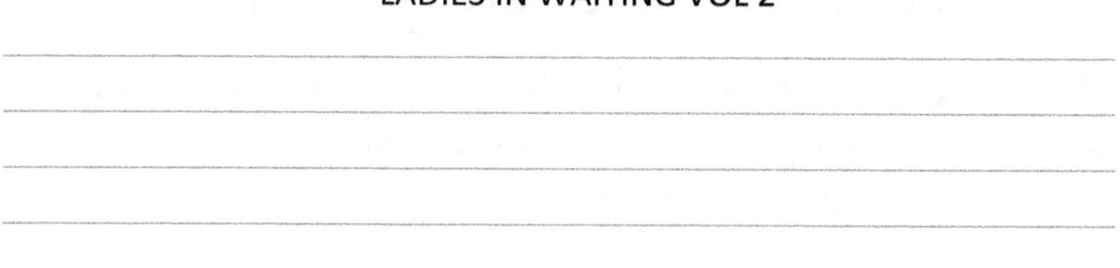

Evaluating the Relationship

Take a step back to evaluate the overall health and dynamics of the relationship objectively. Consider both the positive aspects that strengthen your bond and any recurring issues that cause doubt. Reflect on whether the relationship brings joy, fulfillment, and growth:

Strengths: Identify the qualities and experiences that enhance your connection.

Challenges: Acknowledge areas of conflict or dissatisfaction and discuss how to address them.

Making Informed Decisions

Ultimately, navigating doubt is about making informed decisions that align with your values, needs, and long-term goals. Trust yourself to prioritize your well-being and happiness while considering the impact of your choices on both you and your partner. Seek support from trusted friends, family, or professionals if needed to gain perspective:

Self-Care: Take care of your emotional well-being and prioritize self-reflection.

Consultation: Seek advice from trusted sources to gain perspective.

Growth: Embrace opportunities for personal growth and self-discovery.

Navigating doubt in a relationship requires courage, introspection, and open communication. By listening to your instincts, fostering honest dialogue, and evaluating the relationship's compatibility and dynamics, you can navigate doubts thoughtfully and ultimately make choices that align with your happiness and fulfillment.

Discussion Questions

Understanding Your Doubts:

What are some common sources of doubt in relationships, according to the article? How can identifying these sources help in navigating doubts effectively?

____

____

____

____

____

Reflect on a time when you experienced doubts in a relationship. Were they related to temporary challenges or fundamental issues?

____

____

____

____

____

Reflecting on Your Feelings:

Why is it important to trust your instincts and acknowledge recurring doubts in a relationship? How can journaling or discussing doubts with others help gain clarity?

____

____

Share how you typically assess your feelings in a relationship. What factors do you consider when evaluating the depth of emotional connection and compatibility?

Open and Honest Communication:

Discuss the significance of effective communication in navigating doubts with your partner. How can using "I" statements and active listening improve understanding and resolve conflicts?

Can you recall a time when open communication helped address doubts or concerns in a relationship? What were the outcomes?

Seeking Clarity Together:

Why is seeking clarity as a couple crucial when navigating doubts? What types of questions might facilitate deeper understanding of each other's long-term goals and expectations?

How do you envision having discussions about the future with your partner? What topics would you prioritize to ensure mutual understanding and alignment?

Evaluating the Relationship:

Reflect on the strengths and challenges in your current or past relationships. How did you evaluate these aspects objectively?

What criteria do you believe are essential for determining whether a relationship brings joy, fulfillment, and growth? How can focusing on these criteria help in making informed decisions?

Making Informed Decisions:

Discuss the factors that contribute to making informed decisions in relationships. How do you balance prioritizing your own well-being with considering your partner's feelings and needs?

Share a personal experience where you made a decision about a relationship based on navigating doubts. What lessons did you learn from that experience?

Personal Growth and Support:

How can practicing self-care and seeking support from others contribute to navigating doubts in relationships? What role does personal growth play in gaining clarity and confidence in decision-making?

In what ways can relationships serve as opportunities for personal development and self-discovery, even amidst doubts?

CHAPTER NINE

HEART VS. HEAD: BALANCING EMOTION AND LOGIC

In the realm of decision-making and navigating life's complexities, the interplay between emotions and logic often dictates our choices and outcomes. Whether it's deciding on a career path, managing relationships, or making significant life changes, striking a balance between what the heart desires and what the head logically deduces is crucial. This article explores the dynamic between emotion and reason, offering insights into how to harmonize these sometimes-conflicting aspects of our decision-making process.

Understanding Emotion and Logic

Emotions, driven by our feelings and desires, play a significant role in shaping our perceptions and responses to the world around us. They often guide us towards what we find pleasurable, fulfilling, or comforting. Love, passion, fear, and joy are just a few examples of emotions that can strongly influence our decisions, sometimes leading us to act impulsively or based on immediate gratification.

On the other hand, logic, governed by reason and rationality, helps us analyze situations objectively, weigh pros and cons, and anticipate consequences. Logical thinking involves critical analysis, problem-solving, and strategic planning, aiming for outcomes that are based on evidence, data, and practicality rather than purely on subjective feelings.

The Conflict Between Heart and Head

The conflict between heart and head arises when emotional impulses clash with logical reasoning. For instance, in relationships, the heart may be drawn to someone despite logical reasons suggesting they may not be the best match. Similarly, in career decisions, passion for a particular field may compete with the practical considerations of job stability or financial security.

This conflict can lead to inner turmoil, indecision, and a sense of being torn between what feels right emotionally and what appears right logically. It's essential to recognize that both emotions and logic serve valuable purposes, and finding a balance between the two is key to making well-rounded decisions that align with our long-term goals and values.

Strategies for Balancing Emotion and Logic

Acknowledge Your Emotions: Begin by identifying and understanding your emotions. Recognize how they influence your thoughts and behaviors without immediately acting on them. Journaling or talking to a trusted friend can help clarify your feelings.

Evaluate with Logic: Once you've acknowledged your emotions, engage your logical reasoning. Evaluate the situation objectively by considering facts, potential outcomes, and the implications of your decisions. Ask yourself, "What evidence supports this decision? What are the risks and benefits?"

Seek Perspective: Gain perspective by seeking advice from others who can offer a neutral viewpoint. This can provide insights you may not have considered and help balance emotional biases with rational insights.

Set Priorities and Goals: Define your priorities and long-term goals. This helps prioritize decisions that align with your values and aspirations, ensuring that emotional impulses do not overshadow logical considerations.

Take Time to Decide: Avoid making decisions impulsively. Allow yourself time to process emotions and weigh options carefully. Sleep on important decisions, if possible, as this often brings clarity and reduces the influence of immediate emotional reactions.

Practice Self-Reflection: Regularly reflect on past decisions and their outcomes. Assess how emotions and logic played a role and what you could learn from the experience. Self-awareness helps refine your decision-making process over time.

Benefits of Balanced Decision-Making

Balancing emotion and logic in decision-making offers several benefits:

Reduced Regret: Making decisions that consider both emotional desires and logical reasoning can minimize regrets later.

Enhanced Clarity: Achieving clarity on decisions fosters confidence and peace of mind.

Improved Relationships: Balancing emotions and logic in relationships promotes understanding, effective communication, and mutual respect.

Long-Term Satisfaction: Decisions made with a blend of heart and head often lead to outcomes that are fulfilling in both the short and long term.

Conclusion

Finding the right balance between emotion and logic is a continual journey that requires self-awareness, critical thinking, and a willingness to explore both sides of decision-making. By acknowledging the influence of emotions, harnessing the power of logical reasoning, and striving for alignment with personal values and goals, individuals can navigate life's challenges with greater clarity and purpose. Ultimately, integrating heart and head leads to decisions that are not only well-informed but also resonate deeply with our authentic selves.

Discussion Questions

Certainly! Here are some reflective questions that explore the interplay between emotions and logic in decision-making:

Understanding Emotion and Logic:

How do emotions influence your daily decisions, from small choices to significant life milestones?

Reflect on a recent decision where logical reasoning played a crucial role. How did you weigh facts, evidence, and potential outcomes?

The Conflict Between Heart and Head:

Can you recall a time when you felt torn between following your heart and listening to logical reasoning? How did you navigate this conflict?

In what areas of your life (career, relationships, personal goals) do you find the balance between emotion and logic most challenging?

Strategies for Balancing Emotion and Logic:

When faced with a decision, what steps do you take to acknowledge and understand your emotions before engaging in logical reasoning?

How has seeking perspective from others helped you gain clarity in decision-making, particularly when emotions are strong?

Personal Growth and Learning:

Reflect on a decision where you successfully balance emotions and logic. What were the outcomes? How did this experience contribute to your personal growth?

How do you practice self-reflection to refine your decision-making process over time? What insights have you gained about your own decision-making patterns?

Benefits of Balanced Decision-Making:

Think about a decision that brought long-term satisfaction and fulfillment. How did integrating both emotional desires and logical reasoning contribute to this outcome?

In what ways has achieving clarity in decision-making enhanced your relationships and communication with others?

Applying Balance in Future Decisions:

Looking ahead, how do you envision applying lessons learned about balancing emotion and logic to future decisions?

What are some specific goals or practices you can set to continue refining your ability to harmonize heart and head in decision-making?

CHAPTER TEN
AM I THE ONE? OR SHOULD *HE* LOOK FOR ANOTHER?

Scripture: "For I say, through the grace given to me, to everyone who is among you, not to think of himself more highly than he ought to think, but to THINK SOBERLY......" Romans 12:3a NKJV

Sis,

So, you have checked, double-checked, and even triple-checked off every item on your checklist as you get closer to YOUR big day! Besides, having your Sista squad of matron/maids of honor and bridesmaids causes even more excitement and joy to fill your heart and soul as you get ready to marry the man of your dreams. As anticipation and expectation continues to build surrounding you becoming one with him, there remains ONE lingering question that only YOU can answer with authenticity and transparency while standing in your feminine power.

As we embark upon and navigate through the dating experience toward obtaining and yielding the results of permanent companionship in marriage, we have been conditioned to ask the question: "Is He THE ONE?" "Lord, is he, My husband?" However, the Holy Spirit wants to present an even more intriguing inquiry which requires a greater depth of soul work and revelation on our part. Ask yourself, *"Am I THE ONE? Or should HE look for another?"*

Yes, Holy Spirit is challenging you to get to an internal place of serenity and sobriety for a time of introspection and reflection. Ask yourself: Do I possess the competence and prowess to function and operate as his wife and Kingdom partner in life? Are I prepared and ready in every aspect to take on the requirements of the INSTITUTION of marriage, or am I intoxicated with the IMAGE of marriage? Am I THE ONE equipped to manage within marriage:

the SUCCESSES and the STORMS?

the FAVOR and the FIRE?

the CELEBRATION and the CRUSHING?

the TRIUMPHS and the TRIALS?

the PERKS and the PRESSURE?

the REWARDS and the RESPONSIBILITIES?

the ELEVATION and the EVOLUTION?

the VALLEYS and the VICTORIES?
the WINS, WORK, and WEIGHT?

In the days and years ahead, it is my prayer that through your partnership with Holy Spirit, He will give strength, clarity, insight, admonition, and discipline through the lens of love and truth!

So, Queen, I decree and declare that you are THE ONE distinctly designed and crafted for your mate. Due to your submission of the Father's perpetual transformative architectural work within your heart, mind, soul, and spirit, I also decree that your mate will NOT have to look for another. Why? Because you are THE ONE! Congratulations!

Discussion Questions

Self-Reflection and Preparedness:

How do you personally define being "THE ONE" in the context of marriage and partnership?

What specific qualities and traits do you believe are necessary to be a successful partner in a marriage?

In what ways have you prepared yourself emotionally, mentally, and spiritually for marriage?

Internal Assessment:

Reflect on a time when you had to handle both success and storm in your life. How did you manage each situation, and what did you learn from those experiences?

How do you balance the favor and fire (blessings and challenges) in your current life?

Consider the concept of "celebration and crushing." How do you plan to celebrate your partner's successes while also supporting them during their low points?

Marriage Realities:

What are your thoughts on the idea of being intoxicated with the image of marriage versus being prepared for the reality of it?

Discuss the different aspects of marriage listed in the text (e.g., triumphs and trials, perks, and pressure). Which of these do you feel most confident in managing? Which do you feel might be challenging for you?

How do you envision handling the valleys and victories in your marital journey?

Spiritual and Emotional Readiness:

How do you involve the Holy Spirit in your journey towards marriage readiness? Can you share specific practices or prayers that help you with this?

In what ways has your faith shaped your understanding and expectations of marriage?

How do you maintain a balance between seeking divine guidance and taking practical steps in preparing for marriage?

Personal Growth and Evolution:

How have you evolved personally throughout your dating and engagement journey?

What are some areas in your life where you still see room for growth and improvement before entering marriage?

How do you plan to continue your personal development after getting married?

Vision for the Future:

What is your vision for your marriage, and how does it align with your current understanding of being "THE ONE" for your partner?

How do you plan to contribute to the elevation and evolution of your marriage and partnership?

What steps are you taking to ensure that both you and your partner grow together in your marriage?

Support and Community:

How important is the role of your "Sista squad" (friends, matron/maids of honor, bridesmaids) in your journey towards marriage?

In what ways can your community support you in becoming and being "THE ONE" for your partner?

How do you balance advice and opinions from loved ones with your personal and spiritual convictions?

Practical Considerations:

How do you plan to handle the "wins, work, and weight" of marriage in practical terms?

What strategies do you have for maintaining a healthy work-life balance within your marriage?

How do you and your partner plan to address and manage responsibilities and challenges together?

BIO

 Dr. Varenda S. Williams is a modern-day champion of truth, intercessor, activist, advocate, strategist, solutionist, and a sought-after speaker at both international and national conferences. She is an Amazon #1 Best Seller, a seasoned math and science educational facilitator, and a dynamic leader whom God is using to inspire, train, and guide Kingdom leadership. Dr. Williams is the author of "For Her Majesty's Eyes Only: Confessions Fit for the Marketplace Queen" and a ten-time co-author. With over twenty years of experience in education and more than thirty years in ministry, she currently resides in Houston, Texas.

Email: drladyprof@gmail.com
Facebook: https://www.facebook.com/varenda.williams